The Holy Grail: The History and Legend of the Famous Relic

By Charles River Editors

The tapestry known as *The Achievement of the Grail*

About Charles River Editors

Charles River Editors was founded by Harvard and MIT alumni to provide superior editing and original writing services, with the expertise to create digital content for publishers across a vast range of subject matter. In addition to providing original digital content for third party publishers, Charles River Editors republishes civilization's greatest literary works, bringing them to a new generation via ebooks.

Introduction

The Damsel of the Sanct Grael, **by Dante Gabriel Rossetti (1874)**

The Holy Grail

"And He took a cup and when He had given thanks He gave it to them saying 'Drink this, all of you; for this is My blood of the covenant, which is poured out for many for the forgiveness of sins. I tell you, I shall not drink again of the fruit of the vine until I drink it new with you in My Father's kingdom.'" – Matthew 26:27

"The Grail is the womb of the beloved." – Robert Anton Wilson

The Holy Grail is one of the most famous relics of Christianity, but also one of the least understood. Today, it is mostly associated with Christ's Last Supper, possibly used during the meal as a serving cup. The gospels in the New Testament specifically mention the Holy Chalice that Jesus used to serve wine, so it's no surprise that images of the Holy Grail depict a similar kind of cup. Initially, the Holy Chalice was a separate tradition, but over time, the Holy Grail has come to be indistinguishable from the Holy Chalice itself, a concept that probably would have been foreign to the earliest Christians. While churches throughout Christendom were familiar with traditions regarding the Holy Chalice and some even claimed to have the venerated object, the legend of the Holy Grail was given life during the Middle Ages through folklore. .

Today, the legends written about the Holy Grail are better known than the traditions surrounding the Holy Chalice. The Holy Grail is a prevalent theme in the Arthurian tales, and it eventually became linked to other events in the crucifixion narrative by subsequent legends, including the belief that Joseph used the Holy Grail to catch some of Christ's blood after he was crucified and was being interred. Conveniently, the British writers who wrote of the legend related the tale of how special protectors of the relic brought it to Britain, a simple but effective way of boosting the legitimacy and prestige of the motherland.

While the Arthurian tales about Galahad and Perceval continue to fascinate readers, and the concept of undertaking an arduous quest to attain the Holy Grail has become a secular part of the modern lexicon, scholarly debate also arose over the actual history of the relic. Given the passage of time, and the addition of the literature surrounding it, it should come as no surprise that the historical debate continues today. In addition to the Christian traditions, scholars have looked for other sources that might have influenced the beliefs and legends about the Holy Grail, including searching Celtic mythology and literature, all in an attempt to better understand the emergence of the Holy Grail legend.

The Holy Grail: The History and Legend of the Famous Relic chronicles the legends and theories about the famous holy relic, examining the historical record to piece together an understanding of the known and unknown about the Grail. Along with pictures and a bibliography, you will learn about the Holy Grail like you never have before, in no time at all.

Introductory Note

Much of the information contained in this book draws heavily on two scholarly accounts of the history of the Grail legend. The first is a fairly recent account (2004) written by Richard Barber, who is a visiting professor at the University of York in England. The second is a series of seven articles written at the turn of the last century by William Wells Newell, a folklorist who was a professor at Harvard. To avoid a preponderance of citations of the same two sources, information that is not otherwise credited relies on one of these two sources.

The Creation of the Novel

One of the artifacts alleged to be the Holy Grail in Valencia, Spain. Photo by Madder

At first blush, it would make sense to assume that any description of the Holy Grail and the Grail legend would begin with the crucifixion of Jesus in the early first century A.D., but there is actually no mention of any grail in the Biblical texts or in the writings of the early church fathers. In fact, if someone was able to take a time machine and travel back to around 1000 A.D., during the so-called "Dark Ages", and ask a Christian priest or monk to explain the "Holy Grail", they would have no idea what they were being asked. That's because the grail first appeared not in the Holy Land around Jerusalem during the 1st century, but in 12th century France.

During the course of the 11th and 12th centuries, a new social class of knights had formed. This new social class was well-educated able to read and write, but they were not directly involved in politics or in commerce and trade, as were many of the other upper-class noble citizens of their day. At the same time, this new social class seemed to capture the imagination of scholars and monks, meaning they somehow had one foot squarely in the religious sphere as a religious order while also having the other foot firmly established in the secular world, immersed as they were in court life.

It didn't take long before the more traditional scholars and monks began to envision a virtuous ideal for these knights, captured in the concept of chivalry. The monks' lives were governed by their three-pronged vows of poverty, chastity and obedience, and they struggled to imagine how this new class of knights, who were not bound by such vows, could still live honorable lives pleasing to God, to whom they were nonetheless committed. Rather than writing philosophical treaties about what qualities a knight should possess, they turned to telling stories.

The knights were certainly not poor, given that they wore suits of armor that cost a handsome sum of money and embraced the latest court fashions, but the scholars envisioned a virtuous ideal that a knight would never accept a monetary reward for their deeds. For this reason, most knights needed to come from wealth, and in this way, knights would distinguish themselves from mercenaries and would fight to protect the kingdom or a lady or to preserve their own honor in the case of rival challengers. This new social class was also by no means celibate like the monks. The scholars imagined that they could court ladies and seek their affection as long as they always treated the ladies with the utmost respect. Obedience was even less of a leap, and the knights were thought to be obedient to all who were in authority over them, especially the king or other rulers. And of course, in addition to these ideals, there was a military ideal added to the mix. Knights were supposed to protect those who could not protect themselves, which applied to the church, to women and children, and even to unarmed knights.

The scholars and monks who envisioned this hybrid between the ideal military leader and ideal religious figure needed to find some locus where these new ideals could be conveyed in the form of a story, and the Arthurian legends provided the perfect vehicle for conveying these new concepts. At this time, a very popular book was circulating entitled, *Historia Regum Brittanniae* ("History of the Kings of Britain"), in which Geoffrey of Monmouth wrote of an ancient King Arthur and the tales of his exploits in Britain against the Roman armies. Since Geoffrey claimed that his book was actually a Latin translation of an ancient book written in the British language, many who read it considered it a true book of history." In Geoffrey's work, the Arthurian legend was already quite robust. In it, Arthur appears as a valiant king fighting the Roman army along with his queen, Guinevere, his seneschal Sir Kay, his butler Bedevere, and his nephews Gawain and Mordred. Arthur's father, Uther Pendragon, and the magician Merlin also appear in

Geoffrey's work, but some of the literary themes that would later be associated with Arthur, like the Round Table and the Lady of the Lake, had not yet been developed.

This medieval illustration depicts Merlin reading his prophecies to Vortigern. The illustration appeared in Geoffrey's *Prophetiae Merlini* circa the mid-13th century.

In any case, since Geoffrey used the new social class of knights as a means to describe Arthur and those around him, like his butler and his seneschal, the seeds were already sown. This gave the scholars an opportunity to tell stories about famous knights of a bygone era, who either embodied those ideal virtues or who struggled in their attempt to achieve them. In addition to the religious literature that these medieval scholars read and worked with, there was also the classical Greek and Latin literature that formed the backbone of medieval scholarly education. This literature was replete with legends and myths of heroes who personified various Greek and Roman ideals, and thus this literature was also used as a template for the stories written by the new breed of medieval scholars

Although they told stories, the form they used to tell them was poetry. This milieu gave the scholars a subject on which to focus, the ancient knights old (Arthurian era), and the mode in which to tell the stories, poetic narratives. Since these tales were intended for a wider audience than monks and scholars, they wrote these poetic narratives in their native French rather than in Latin. In a sense, these poetic tales marked the inception of the modern genre of the fiction novel.

The Grail as a Paten (Dish)

The actual story of the Grail begins with the French writer Chrétien de Troyes, whose name is the French equivalent of Christian of Troy in English. Troyes was the town in north-central France where he lived, and he was a prolific writer of this new genre of the novel that focused on the exploits of knights. Chrétien was one of the first of these scholars who created an entirely new genre of literature by taking the idea that the individuals who surrounded Arthur were knights and running with it. It was Chrétien who added some of the most famous wrinkles of the Arthurian legend, including the characters Lancelot and Perceval, and it was also Chrétien who developed the theme of a romantic affair between Lancelot and Guinevere.

Lancelot became the most famous figure introduced by Chrétien, but it was in his introduction of the knight Perceval that the Grail quest originates. In one of his earliest works, Chrétien had mentioned Perceval in passing as a knight in King Arthur's court, but he had not elaborated on this character at all. It was only in Chrétien's last novel, *The Story of the Grail*, commissioned by Philip, Count of Flanders, that the figure of Perceval truly comes to life. This work actually told the heroic tale of two knights, Gawain and Perceval. In it, Chrétien described Perceval as a boy who suffered grievous loss in his childhood with the deaths of his father and older brothers in their knightly quests. As a result, his mother tries desperately to shield the child from the dangerous life of the knights. She fled into the forest, where she raised Perceval not as a child of means but as a Welsh rustic, far from the temptations of court life.

However, while out hunting in the forest one day, Perceval comes across a group of knights traveling through the region. Fascinated by their attire and weapons, he asks in great detail about each of the weapons they carry, including their proper names and purpose, as well as how and where they acquired them. The knights kindly answer his questions, informing him in the course of their answers that King Arthur is the source of most of their equipment. He immediately becomes enamored with the possibility of pursuing life as a knight, much to his mother's chagrin. Resigned to the fact that she will not be able to dissuade him, his mother teaches him about proper etiquette, proper conduct around women, and some religion. He then leaves home to appear before King Arthur, where he plans to demand knighthood for himself. An interesting side note in this story is that the location of Arthur's court in Camelot has yet to be established in the tradition when Chrétien wrote his story. Therefore, the city to which Perceval travels to find Arthur at court is Carlisle.

Along his journey to Arthur's court, Perceval comes upon a girl alone in a tent. Forgetting everything that his mother had taught him, he steals a kiss from her and takes a ring from her as a memento for the occasion. This leaves her in hot water with her lover, who arrives on the scene after Perceval has obliviously gone his merry way. Her lover is convinced that she has been unfaithful to him and has given tokens of her affection to a rival lover.

Perceval finally makes it to Arthur's court amongst much mockery, but he then bests another knight and dons his armor. He also finds a mature knight to mentor him in weaponry, and he defends the lady of a castle from an unwelcome suitor, ultimately falling for her himself. Perceval had only met the damsel in distress on his way to check on his mother, so although he has now found love with this woman, he insists on resuming his original journey to check on the health and well-being of his mother, promising his beloved that he would return in short order.

Medieval illustration depicting Perceval

It is at this point that the adventure involving the Grail begins. Perceval arrives at a river where he meets two men fishing in a boat, and he immediately recognizes that the river is too deep and strong for him to cross on horseback. He calls to the men and asks whether there is any type of bridge or other means that he might use to cross the river. Dejected, he then follows up his question with another as to where he might find lodging for the night. The fisherman offers to put Perceval up in his house for the night and directs Perceval where to find his house. After some initial difficulty, Perceval finds the house, which turns out to be a magnificent castle set back in a valley in the woods. As soon as he crosses the drawbridge, attendants appear ready to take his armor, care for his horse and provide him a fresh change of clothes. They escorted him to his room, where he rests for awhile until he is summoned to see the lord of the castle.

The attendants escort him into the great hall of the castle, where he sees a nobleman reclining before a great fireplace. He approaches and introduces himself to the lord of the castle, the fisherman who had invited him, and he learns that the lord is beset with some type of injury that greatly restricts his mobility. They talk for a while about Perceval's journey during the day, only to be interrupted by another attendant carrying a large fine sword. The attendant explains to his lord that it is a present from the latter's niece. The master craftsman who made it is now on his deathbed, so it will be one of only three that this craftsman has ever made. She asks that her lord re-gift it to someone who would make good use of it, since the physical disability now affecting her lord would prevent him from being able to use it. The lord thanks his attendant and then immediately takes the scabbard and wraps it around Perceval's waist, stating that he has decided to give it to him because it was destined for him. Perceval thanks the lord of the castle and draws the sword, deftly testing its balance before returning it to its scabbard. He then removes the scabbard and hands it to the attendant, who had been entrusted with the rest of his armor.

Perceval then returns to his seat and continues his conversation with the lord of the castle. They talk well into the evening and enjoy a splendid conversation, but while they are speaking something odd happens. First, one of the attendants enters the great hall from one of the chambers carrying a white lance upright around its middle. The boy proceeds with the lance in between the fire and the lounge in which they are sitting. As he does so, a drop of blood emerges from the tip of the lance and trickles down the weapon to the boy's hand. He watches in awe and amazement at the sight and longs to ask the lord of the castle about it, but then he remembers the instructions of his mentor. His mentor had warned him sternly to beware of talking too much. Perceval convinces himself that this is such an occasion when he should keep his mouth shut.

Perceval and the lord continue conversing, but shortly thereafter, four more attendants enter the hall. Two boys enter first, carrying large candelabras, followed by a beautiful girl who carries a grail, who is then followed by another girl carrying a silver trencher. Upon entering the room, the reflected light gleaming from the grail is so bright that the light from the individual candles becomes indiscernible. These four also walk in a procession that leads between the fire and the lounge. Yet again, although Perceval is dying to ask questions about the grail and trencher, the warning of his mentor again echoes in his mind, causing him to remain quiet. He decides it would be best to ask his question the next morning, when he can direct it to one of the servants so as not to bother the lord of the castle with such a question. At this point, the narrator provides an aside informing the reader that virtue requires a balance between talking too much and not asking the appropriate questions.

The two spend the rest of evening feasting on the most delicious food and wine that one can imagine. After each course of their meal, the lance and grail pass by in a similar fashion. When they are finally exhausted after making a long evening of it, they each retire to bed, with the servants carrying the lord of the castle to his bedroom upon a blanket.

The next morning, Perceval wakes up with the rest of the household clearly awake, but finding no servants around to attend to him. The story takes on an almost comical tone as the knight attempts, with great difficulty, to dress himself. Once dressed, he then wanders about the areas of the castle with which he is familiar, calling out and making a loud raucous, but he can find no one. He then steps outside to find his horse saddled with his lance and shield leaning against the wall, clearly prepared for him to leave. He then rides over to the drawbridge and finds it lowered, so he thinks to himself that the servants must have gone to check their traps in the woods. The narrator informs the reader, however, that it had been lowered specifically to allow him to leave at whatever time he wished. Perceval then rides across the drawbridge in an effort to find the servants and ask his as yet unanswered questions regarding the Grail and the lance. Before he has even crossed the bridge it begins to rise and Perceval has to jump his horse in order to clear the last stretch. He is greatly puzzled by this behavior and calls back to the castle asking to speak to whoever raised the bridge while he was yet crossing it. But call and call as he might, he receives no reply.

On the road from the castle he sees hoof-prints that he takes to belong to someone from the castle. He follows them in an effort to ask his remaining questions, but after a distance down the road, the hoof-prints fade and disappear. As he continues down the road, he happens upon a woman weeping over a decapitated knight. He offers to help in whatever capacity he can, as is the duty of any honorable knight, and they begin a conversation. As they are talking, the woman is taken aback by the great condition of his horse since there is no habitation for many miles in either direction. Perceval argues with the woman that she must be mistaken because he found shelter in a very large castle only a few miles away. The woman then realizes what must have happened and explains to Perceval that it was the Fisher King who offered him hospitality. She explains that he received his injuries when a javelin shot through both his hips preventing him from being able to mount his horse any longer. The only activity that he continues to enjoy is fishing in the river, which is why folks now call him the "Fisher King." Had he asked the questions that were so prominent in his mind, the Fisher King would have been healed. Only now, evil will befall himself and others for his inconsiderate behavior.

The woman then asks the knight his name, and it is only at this point in the story that Chrétien provides the name of the knight for the first time: Perceval the Welshman. Although she doesn't quite understand why he calls himself a Welshman (this was, after all, his mother's pretense), she informs him that she is none other than his cousin. When she realizes the close relation, it dawns on her that he may not be aware of his mother's death. She informs him that his leaving home suddenly seems to have caused her early death.

When all hope seems to be lost, Perceval's fortune finally changes. He meets up with the girl whose ring he had stolen and restores it to her, explaining to her lover that he was the one who acted inappropriately and that her lover has nothing to worry about in regards to the faithfulness of his girl. Perceval also has the opportunity to restore his honor before Arthur's seneschal Sir Kay, who had been the source of most of the teasing and ribbing he received at Arthur's court when he had sought knighthood. He accomplished this by unseating Sir Kay from his horse while he is daydreaming.

Ultimately, however, Perceval's good fortune does not last long. An ugly woman comes to Perceval and chastises him for keeping his mouth shut at the home of the Fisher King. It is because of him that the Fisher King will now never be healed of his wounds and, therefore, will no longer be able to protect his country. The helpless members of his kingdom will now only multiply, all due to the indifference of Perceval. Upon hearing this news, Perceval is overcome with grief and makes the following vow: until he learns the cause for the bleeding lance and the identity of the one being served by the ornate chalice (grail) and dish, he will never sleep in the same house twice, nor will he turn away from this adventure, no matter how perilous.

At this point, Chrétien turns his attention to Gawain and his adventures, and the stories of the two knights begin to converge when Gawain is sent on a quest for the bleeding lance. When Chrétien returns his focus to Perceval, some five years have passed since the reader last heard about Perceval. During that time, he has been questing for secrets to the lance and grail mysteries, completely absent from any companionship provided by Arthur's court or from his beloved. He has become consumed with battle and has lost all track of time or seasons; the corollary to this is that he has forgotten God. Adrift from any religious figures or sacred places, he has not observed the most holy of Christian holidays nor attended mass regularly as a proper knight should.

One day, while riding in the wilderness, he meets a band of pilgrims clad in woolen garments as a sign of penitence. The leader of this group of pilgrims, who consists primarily of knights and ladies, proceeds to lambast Perceval for donning full armor on the day when Christ died. Perceval, oblivious of time, had been completely unaware that it was Good Friday. He also informs Perceval that they have just come from making confession and receiving absolution from a hermit in a cell up the road. With a repentant heart, Perceval takes the road the pilgrims had come down and finds the chapel of the hermit. Perceval makes a confession to the hermit and in the process he learns that the hermit is his uncle. He also learns the identity of the one served by the Grail. The occupant of the room of the castle into which the servants had carried these vessels was none other than the hermit's brother and the father of the Fisher King. The hermit explains to Perceval that the reason he was struck dumb before the Fisher King was a result of his impudence in leaving his mother so suddenly, which caused her death.

The hermit then proceeds to provide more information about the Fisher King's father. He had spent the past 20 years (or 12 years according to some manuscripts) isolated in that room, receiving no food aside from a consecrated wafer carried in the Grail. The Grail is such a holy thing that the host carried in it both comforts and sustains his life. The hermit then offers Perceval absolution for his sins, and Perceval remains with the hermit until Easter.

At this point, Chrétien turns again to Gawain and promises to return later in the narrative to Perceval, but he died before finishing his story. It was published in this uncompleted form, and many later writers attempted to finish the story, but none of these have satisfied most readers.

Before his death, Chrétien described the features of the Grail in *The Story of the Grail*. The Grail was gold, richly ornamented, and was a dish in which food (in this case, a wafer) was served. That said, it's also clear that the main focus in the story was the spiritual nature of the man the Grail served, not the Grail itself. The story says nothing of the Grail's origin; in fact, Chrétien appeared to have been drawing on a legend about the ascetic monk Pachomius, who was miraculously able to sustain himself by consuming only a wafer a day. It's also important to understand that this wafer was simply food and had nothing to do with the holy rite of communion, which is made clear by the fact that a young servant girl carries the Grail in the story, which is how kings and noblemen were fed. Since the Grail was not being carried by a priest, the only people who served Holy Communion, it's apparent that Chrétien was not suggesting the Fisher King's father was taking communion. There is also no mention of any wine in the story.

An icon of Saint Pachomius, who's now remembered as the Father of Spiritual Communal Monastic Life

Some later commentators maintained that the bleeding lance in the story, which is the focus of Gawain's quest, is meant to evoke the spear that pierced Christ's side during his crucifixion, but others, including those who tried to finish Chrétien's story, made no such connection. Since Gawain is on a quest for the lance, the idea of most subsequent writers was that he would then pick up this weapon for his own use, in the way Arthur finds and wields Excalibur. If that was the case, the spear used at the crucifixion would hardly be considered appropriate for a knight to brandish. Brown has shown clear connections between this lance, as Chrétien describes it, and a poisonous lance in Irish tradition held in a magical fairy castle that would be dipped in a cauldron of blood (Brown, 1910, 17-19).

Regardless of how readers perceive the bleeding lance and the Grail in Chrétien's work, they appear quite devoid of any of the Christian religious symbolism that is so integral to the later stories regarding the grail. Moreover, whatever the actual shape Chrétien envisioned for the Grail in his work, it was certainly more of a paten (a dish or plate) than a chalice or cup.

The Derrynaflan Paten was a medieval dish used as part of a communion set

The Grail as a Table

The next main player in the development of the Grail legend was Robert de Boron. It is clear from dedications in other works of his that he worked for Gautier de Montbéliard, and this relationship between Robert and Gautier is significant for several reasons. First, Gautier was connected by marriage to the counts of Champagne and Flanders, which helps to establish his access to Chrétien's work. Gautier was also involved in the Fourth Crusade, which took him to Cyrus, where he ruled as regent. Some scholars have also suggested that Robert de Boron accompanied his lord to the Holy Land and Cyprus, where he would have been exposed to many of the Oriental influences that are apparent in his work. It is more likely, however, that he remained in Montbéliard, near his hometown of Boron, since his work had such an impact on the further development of the Grail legend in this northern region of France.

Whereas Chrétien de Troyes looked to the Classical Greek and Latin tradition for influence on the style of *The Story of the Grail*, Robert de Boron was more indebted to the Lives of the Saints and different apocryphal Gospels that scholars were translating into French during his day. During the 12th century, these works had become quite popular throughout the monasteries of France, so he would not have needed to travel far to be strongly influenced by them. Robert de Boron took the ideas that he saw outlined by Chrétien in his novel-style and re-imagined them in line with the Lives of the Saints, a work he was more comfortable and familiar with.

Robert de Boron conceived of his work as a sort of prequel to *The Story of the Grail*, which he aptly named *The History of the Grail*, but since he also supplied his own version of the Perceval story, it would also be fair to call Robert de Boron's work a literary reboot. To understand how Robert de Boron transformed the imagery found in Chrétien's work, it is necessary to be familiar with the physical characteristics of some of the religious paraphernalia during the 12th century. The paten was the Latin name of the serving plate used to hold the host (bread or wafer) portion of the communion rite. These plates were round and had 6, 8 or 12 indentations, almost like the petals of a flower molded along the outer edge that would serve to separate any food that was placed into it. The church altars at this time had similar petal-like indentations surrounding their outer rim. Although most altars were square in shape, there were certainly round altars of this type in churches in the region as well. The shape of the paten and the shape of the round altar bears striking similarities, and it is likely that when Robert read Chrétien's *The Story of the Grail* and how it described the Grail, he pictured a paten with a wafer like the communion host served on it. Nevertheless, when he envisioned his grand Grail saga, Robert transformed the paten into a dining table, the secular equivalent of the altar. (Barb, 1956, 40-67).

A paten next to a chalice. Picture by Andreas Püttmann

Robert begins his Grail reboot by describing a "vessel" on which Jesus broke the bread with his disciples at the Last Supper. As he describes this vessel, the reader can picture a paten similar to that described by Chrétien, but there is also nothing stopping the reader from interpreting this vessel as the table itself upon which Jesus and the disciples ate. This vessel holds the original communion bread, in the same manner that the Grail held the host for the Fisher King's father.

Once he has made this connection for his readers with the imagery he uses, Robert is then free to lead his readers off on a path of his own choosing. When the Jews came to arrest Jesus in the garden, one of them took that vessel (or table) from the house near where they were staying after searching it. This Jewish religious leader then gave the vessel to Pontius Pilate, who got rid of it by offering it to Joseph of Arimathea, in accordance with his desire to "wash his hands" of the entire affair. When Joseph took Jesus' body down from the cross and washed it in preparation for burial, he collected the blood that flowed from Jesus' wounds in this same vessel.

Given the progression of Robert's narrative, the idea of the Grail being a small paten becomes incongruous with the story. After all, if Joseph is busy washing and preparing the body of Jesus, why or how would he be holding a paten to catch the blood that flowed out of his wounds. On the other hand, if Robert is talking about an altar type low table, this would be ideal for washing a body, and the impressions already set in the table would automatically collect the blood flowing from the body's wounds.

When the Roman's learned that Jesus' body had gone missing, they immediately suspected Joseph of Arimathea since it was his tomb, and they threw him in prison. It was while he was languishing in prison that Jesus appeared to Joseph and explained that he had risen from the dead. As is common in apocryphal Gospels, he then went on to explain the significance behind each of the elements in the modern (13th century) communion rite. It is here where Robert de Boron most clearly articulates the imagery upon which he is drawing for this story, and his wording is important in this regard.

> "Joseph, you took me from the cross. And you know well that I took the Last Supper at the house of Simon the Leper, where I said that I was to be betrayed. As I said at that *table*, several *tables* will be established in my service, to make the sacrament in my name, which will be a reminder of the cross; the *vessel* of the sacrament will be a reminder of the stone tomb in which you laid me, and the *paten* which will be placed on top will be a reminder of the lid with which you covered me, and the cloth called the corporal will be a reminder of the winding-sheet in which you wrapped me." (*Joseph d'Arimathie*, 110-11, emphasis added)

Here Jesus explains to Joseph the significance of elements that will be used in the rite of communion for centuries to come. The first item Jesus mentions is the "vessel," which is the term used all along for the object that Robert will later identify directly as the Grail. This "vessel" corresponds to the stone tomb. It becomes even more confusing as Jesus continues his lesson in the symbolism of the objects, when he mentions the paten as a reminder of the lid used to seal the tomb, but the paten is the plate or dish on which the host rests. If the host is on the paten, what is the role of the 'vessel' that is clearly under the paten? The clear answer is that the term "vessel" Robert de Boron has been using in his poem refers to a table or altar; it is this table upon which the paten itself rests. The stone or marble material of the "vessel" evokes the stone tomb in which Jesus was entombed. This identification also clarifies the introductory lines that refer to several tables where the sacramental service will be established. The cloth (*corporal*) is then the linen-type napkin that is often folded around the bread or wafers to keep it pure (from bugs and insects) until it can be served.

Robert then refers to additional secret knowledge, another common theme in apocryphal Gospels. He claims he learned this secret knowledge from reading a book detailing the conversation between the risen Jesus and Joseph of Arimathea that he is unable to share with the reader. He calls this book *The High Book of the Grail*. After the Romans release Joseph from prison, he gathers around him a group of disciples and they collectively guard the vessel. When they begin to sin, their crops fail and they suffer a famine. The risen Jesus then tells Joseph to prepare a table similar to the Last Supper on which he will put the "vessel", the idea here being that the "vessel" tabletop would then fit seamlessly over the ordinary table. Jesus then instructs Joseph to cover the "vessel" with a tablecloth, which would leave it unseen by the disciples, an important thing for the events that follow. If this was a vessel of a different shape than a table, like a chalice or a plate, it would most likely be clearly seen by Joseph's disciples and could not achieve the desired effect.

The worthy disciples are invited to sit at the table, while the unworthy are excluded. Those seated at the table become filled with a sense joy and fulfillment, despite being unaware of the immediate presence of the "vessel," whereas those left standing felt nothing. The group seated then discussed with each other what they should call this vessel. One among their group, Petrus, declared, "Those who wish to call it rightly will call it the Grail (*graal*), which gives joy and delight (*agréer*) to those who can stay in its presence that they feel as elated as a fish escaping from a man's hands into the wide water." (Barber, 2004, 42).

Robert then proceeds to trace the history of the Grail from Joseph to his brother-in-law Bron, who took the title Fisher King and whose followers became "the company of the Grail." A few centuries pass, and master Blaise, a disciple of Merlin, takes up the task of recording the deeds of Arthur and his court, as well as those of "the company of the Grail." He also describes how Merlin encouraged Uther Pendragon, Arthur's father, to establish the Round Table. In this part, Robert de Boron draws on a fairly recent tradition introduced by Wrace in his Norman translation of Geoffrey of Monmouth's *Historia Regum Brittanniae*, managing to connect the Grail directly to Arthur's court by means of the Round Table. The Round Table now becomes a picture of the Grail, which also places it firmly within a Christian context. Merlin then warns Arthur that he will not become emperor of Rome until one of his knights is able to enter the court of the Fisher King and ask who the Grail serves. Those questions will heal the Fisher King and remove the curse under which Britain has languished for many years.

With that background, the stage is set for the adventures of Perceval at the Grail castle, which Robert de Boron recounts in much the same way as they appear in Chrétien's account. When Perceval leaves the hermit's chapel, he participates in a large tournament, and Merlin approaches him that night in disguise and chastises him for not keeping his vow about not remaining more than one night in the same place. This galvanizes Perceval to continue his quest, which takes him another year to complete. He finally arrives at the mystical Grail castle again, and this time he asks his questions about the nature of the processional objects as soon as they enter his view. As soon as the question leaves his mouth, the Fisher King transforms before his eyes, healed of his previous infirmities. The honor of "Keeper of the Grail" then passes to Perceval, who also learns from the Fisher King before he dies the secret words Jesus related to Joseph of Arimathea. After that, Robert de Boron concludes his story of Arthur, but little more is said about the fate of the Grail.

The Grail as a Levitating Cornucopia

After Chrétien's death, his uncompleted poem spread like wildfire as it was copied and recopied by scribes throughout France. The popularity of this new genre, written in vernacular French rather than Latin, was revolutionary, and the fact that this literary masterpiece remained incomplete made it even more popular. Scholars clamored to write the definitive ending to this tale, and in time, Philip's children and grandchildren commissioned other writers to finish what Chrétien had started, but each effort was so unsatisfactory that subsequent rulers continued to re-commission writers to finish the work. In the end, the four most prominent continuations were attached to Chrétien's work and circulated with it.

The first two continuations were attached in order. *The First Continuation* was written either in Burgundy or Champagne, but the name of the author and the circumstances under which he wrote this continuation have been lost to history. Jeanne, Countess of Flanders and Philip's granddaughter, commissioned Wauchier de Denain to write *The Second Continuation* and also commissioned Manessier to write *The Third Continuation*. However, because what would have been *The Fourth Continuation* (written by Gerbert de Montreuil) was also designed to follow *The Second Continuation* and because its conclusion was not nearly as gratifying the work written by Manessier, it was inserted before Manessier's work with the concluding lines of *The Second Continuation* being reduplicated at the end of Gerbert de Montreuil's work to provide a suitable transition.

Each continuation takes the Grail myth in a different direction. For the anonymous author of the first continuation, Perceval is no longer the hero or focus of the story. Since Chrétien had turned his attention to the adventures of Gawain when his story was cut off, the first continuation had Gawain making the subsequent visits to the Grail castle and never returned its attention to Perceval. When Gawain visits the Grail castle, he encounters several of the elements that were present in Chrétien's Grail castle. The bleeding lance appears, except this time it is not part of a procession but mounted on a wall, where the blood that flows from its tip pools into a silver vessel and then flows into a channel that leads to an undisclosed location. The Grail appears as well, but it no longer needs to be carried by human hands because it levitates over the dining table on its own accord and produces food and drink in abundance for those dining at the table. The theme of the knight's questions continues in the first continuation, but they are no longer the primary test of the knight's mettle. For Gawain, the primary challenge of the Grail castle lies in a broken sword, which he must try to meld seamlessly back together. Not only does Gawain fail to mend the sword properly, but when he does ask the Fisher King his questions regarding the sword and the bleeding lance, he falls asleep before even hearing the answer to his first question.

The Grail as a Luminescent Mystery

The author of the second continuation is not nearly as mysterious. Jeanne, the granddaughter of Philip of Flanders (who commissioned the Story of the Grail), commissioned Wauchier de

Denain to complete the work, obviously unimpressed with the work of the first continuator. However, Wauchier did not completely dismiss the work of the first continuator but let it stand and added onto the two-part story. Wauchier was what readers would today call a hack writer. He did not have the talent that Chrétien possessed, nor did he even have the skill of the first continuator. Nevertheless, because the first continuator had such divergent ideas about the nature of the Grail and the bleeding lance from those of Chrétien, Wauchier set about the task of harmonizing them.

Wauchier returned his attention to Perceval, as Chrétien had promised to do in his work before he died, and Wauchier added many of his own adventures to his continuing account of Perceval. At the heart of his narrative is a lady in castle with a self-playing chessboard. At one point, Perceval finds himself in the middle of the forest in the dead of night, and while there, he sees in the distance five lights that look to be candles but is not sure what they are. These candles are exceptionally bright and light up the entire forest around them. It is not until the following day that Perceval is informed this light is a sign of the presence of the Grail. His informant surmises that the Fisher King must have been nearby with the Grail. The light that accompanies it is designed to protect those who see it both physically and spiritually from the Devil.

Much later in the story of Perceval's adventures, he again sees a bright light at night, but this time an oak tree looks to be on fire, or as if a thousand candles were burning in its branches. But as he approaches the tree it disappears before his eyes. Then He is led through a whole series of mysterious and miraculous sights until he eventually finds the Grail castle again. The Fisher King welcomes him as he had done during Perceval's first visit to the Grail castle and then listens intently as Perceval recounts the tails of his adventures since he last saw the Fisher King. As before, they sit down to eat dinner, and a procession begins. On this occasion, it actually begins with a beautiful servant girl carrying the Grail, followed by a second beautiful girl carrying the bleeding lance. A servant boy brings up the rear carrying the broken sword mentioned by the first continuator. This time, Perceval does ask about the Grail and the bleeding lance, but instead of answering his questions directly, the Fisher King digresses into a discussion about Perceval's adventures. When Perceval notes that he has yet to hear an answer to his questions, the Fisher King assures him that he will say more about them after they have eaten. He then asks about the broken sword, and the Fisher King gives him the challenge to mend it. His reward for accomplishing the task will be to hear the answer to his questions. As was the case with Gawain, Perceval comes so close, but a notch remains in the sword that Perceval was unable to repair. On that note, Wauchier ended his continuation of the Grail story.

The Grail as Healing Relic

The story of the Grail now contained Chrétien's original and the two continuations. It was this version that was then widely circulated throughout the region of France where they had originated, with multiple copies being made. As such, two different writers took the second continuation as their jumping off point and continued the story from there.

The first writer was Manessier, hired by the same patron who had hired Wauchier: Jeanne, the countess of Flounders. Though she liked what Wauchier had done with the story in his second continuation, she still wanted a sense of closure that Wauchier had not provided. Manessier was more than willing to try his hand at the famous story of the Grail, and to provide some much needed closure. Picking up where Wauchier had left off, Manessier has the Fisher King answer Perceval's questions, since he nearly succeeded in his task. The Fisher King describes the history of the bleeding lance and then passes over any mention of the Grail to focus on the broken sword. This then launches Perceval into another series of adventures. In one such adventure, Perceval unknowingly challenges and fights Lancelot's brother, Ector. The two knock one another unconscious and nearly kill each other. When they come to, an angel has appeared before them holding the Grail. The close proximity to the Grail results in the two being healed of their wounds. At another point in the narrative, Perceval finds himself again at the Grail castle and dines with the Fisher King amidst the procession as Chrétien had described it initially.

During this meal, Perceval learns that the Fisher King is his uncle and that he will one day inherit the kingdom ruled by the Fisher King. Perceval then returns to Camelot until a maiden comes to inform him of his uncle's death. The Grail is part of the coronation ceremony for Perceval and serves the guests, most likely in the manner of the cornucopia described by the anonymous writer of the first continuation. Perceval rules the kingdom for a time, after which he retires to become a hermit, all the while accompanied by the Grail, the bleeding lance and the trencher. When Perceval finally dies, the Grail disappears as well, never to be seen again.

That was the type of closure the countess of Flanders was seeking that was absent from the previous continuations of the Grail story, but while Manessier was busy writing his conclusion to the Grail story, the countess of Pontheiu, who had acquired one of the many copies of the Story of the Grail with the two continuations, commissioned her own writer, Gerbert de Montreuil, to finish the work. Gerbert de Montreuil was a very accomplished writer, but he did not provide the same level of closure that Manessier was able to provide. When later scribes had some manuscripts with Manessier's continuation and others with Gerbert's continuation, they were faced with a choice. Most of the scribes chose to include both by putting Gerbert's continuation first so that the story would end with Manessier's conclusion. To provide a smoother transition, the scribes repeated Wauchier's concluding lines at the end of the second continuation after Gerbert's continuation. Regardless, Gerbert's continuation does not provide any further information about the history or nature of the Grail.

Prose Tales of the Grail

The idea of the novel as a genre continued to develop in tandem with the legend of the Grail, but whereas the initial novel writers wrote in poetic form ala the style of the Classical epic narratives, later writers began to explore prose writing as a more popular means of packaging their novels. The work of Chrétien, Robert de Boron, and the people who had added continuations had all written poetry, but the later Grail traditions appeared in this new prose style. With the introduction of the prose style, the conceptualization of the nature and history of the Grail becomes much more unified than the disparate views presented by the earlier poetic writers.

The Flemish court was enamored with the Grail story, so the Lord of Cambrin commissioned an entirely separate Grail story for his neighbor Jean de Nesle, the castellan of Bruges. The writer of this prose account got a kick out of tweaking Perceval's name to read Perlesvaus, which translates into French as the "loss of Vales." Since the author is unknown, scholars use this unique naming convention as the means of referring to this work, thereby calling it *Perlesvaus*. Unlike the enigmatic way that the poetic writers referred to the Grail, in this work the author defines the grail clearly and concisely in the very first line of his work: "Hear the story of that holy vessel which is called the Grail, in which the precious blood of the Savior was gathered on the day when he was crucified to redeem mankind from Hell: Josephus recorded it…" (*Perlesvaus* I, 23). Here the author summarizes the gist of Robert de Boron's work and adds that it was preserved for perpetuity by the Jewish writer who was a contemporary of Jesus' ministry and crucifixion, Josephus.

Perlesvaus manages to harmonize the various Grail stories that were in circulation in a more profound way than Wauchier had done in the *Second Continuation*. The author begins his story with a shorter recap of the history of the Grail from Joseph of Arimathea up to the time of King Arthur as presented by Robert de Boron. He then proceeds to identify the problem that needs solving as King Arthur's lack of zeal, which can only be accomplished if a knight asks the Fisher King the fated question. After that, the author relates the adventures of three knights in conjunction with the Grail castle. Gawain is the first, and he brings to the Grail castle the sword with which John the Baptist was beheaded as the price of admission. This is a substitute for the broken sword introduced by the first continuation. While at the dining table of the Grail castle, Gawain sees a procession of the Grail and the bleeding lance, but when he looks at the Grail, he sees a chalice inside the Grail, which the narrator highlights as an odd occurrence because there was no chalice in all of Britain at the time. Gawain also sees a vision of Jesus, presented as a king nailed to the cross, but he ultimately fails to ask the fated question and finds himself booted out of the Grail castle. Lancelot is the next knight in the story to have adventures at the Grail castle, but the Grail does not even appear during Lancelot's time at the Grail castle, because of his sinful affair with Queen Guinevere.

The story then introduces the hero, Perlesvaus. He is in the midst of fighting his own uncle, who is the king of Castle Mortal and the sworn enemy of the Fisher King. During this battle, Gawain brings a message from Perlesvaus' sister that their mother is in trouble and needs his help. Perlesvaus defeats his uncle and sails away to help his mother. On his way to Camelot, Perlesvaus picks up the shield of Joseph of Arimathea that had been sent on to Carlisle by the Fisher King. Meanwhile, Perlesvaus' sister has been keeping vigil in a cemetery outside the

Grail castle. One night, evil spirits battle it out in the graveyard and announce at midnight that the Fisher King is dead, the king of Castle Mortal has usurped the throne of the Grail castle, and the Grail is nowhere to be found. Perlesvaus is the only one who can help. Perlesvaus reunites with his sister and mother at the entrance to Camelot, and soon thereafter, Perlesvaus is summoned to the Grail castle. He happens to pass the old hermit (from Chrétien's original story), who reveals the allegorical meaning underlying several of his adventures. Perlesvaus then teams up with a dozen hermits to overthrow his uncle in the Grail castle. He is successful, which causes the Grail, the bleeding lance and the sword used to behead John the Baptist to all reappear in the adjacent chapel.

The author then seeks to unite the various depictions of the Grail into a cohesive story in the following way: "Now the story tells us that at that time there was no chalice in the land of King Arthur. The Grail appeared at the consecration in *five forms*, but they should not be revealed...But Arthur saw all the changes, and last appeared the chalice...The king was filled with joy at what he had seen, and he bore in his heart the memory of the name and form of the holy chalice." (*Perlesvaus* I, 304-5 [emphasis added])

This story clearly acknowledges that up until this point, each author had his own idea of what shape the Grail took. Rather than leaving these as irreconcilable, this author makes that fact integral to the mystery of the Grail, and concludes by canonizing his own image, that of a chalice, as the official shape of the Grail.

One of the longest stories associated with the Grail goes by the name of the *Vulgate Cycle*, or *The Lancelot Grail*. As the name suggests, this Grail story shifts its focus from Perceval to Lancelot, and the cycle originally consisted of a trilogy made up of *Lancelot*, *The Quest of the Holy Grail*, and the *Death of Arthur*. The first book, *Lancelot*, spends a great deal of time establishing Lancelot as the preeminent knight in King Arthur's court. The tale then shifts to Gawain, who arrives at a castle with a moat and a king. There he sees the grail, in the shape of a chalice that acts as the traditional cornucopia, providing the assembled knights food and drink in ample measure. When Gawain fails to pray before his meal because of the beauty of the maiden holding the Grail, he is prohibited from having any of the food the Grail supplies. He is then thrown out of the castle in disgrace and learns that the name of the castle is Corbenic.

Illustration from a medieval manuscript of the Vulgate Cycle

The story returns its focus to Lancelot, who himself makes his way to Corbenic. Unlike Gawain, Lancelot is able to partake of the food that the Grail supplies. Pelles, the King of the Grail castle, has secret knowledge that Lancelot is destined to beget a child with Pelles' daughter, Helaine, who will grow up to free Pelles' kingdom from its curse. Because Pelles knows of Lancelot's love for Guinevere, Pelles has Brisane, Helaine's tutor, serve Lancelot a magical drink that will make him see Guinevere when he looks at Helaine. The ruse works, and Lancelot sleeps with Helaine, impregnating her. The next morning, Lancelot is disgusted with their trickery, but by that point he can do nothing about it.

Lancelot then introduces another knight into the Grail story: Bors de Ganis, the cousin of Lancelot. Bors subsequently visits Corbenic to feast on the food provided by the Grail, which he does twice, and on the second visit, he meets Helaine along with Lancelot's son. It is not until the end of *Lancelot* that the author reveals the name of the son to be Galahad. The story at last introduces Perceval, who fights Ector, Lancelot's brother, as in Manessier's continuation. Again, like Manessier's continuation, the Grail appears before them and heals them of their wounds.

The Quest of the Holy Grail begins with Galahad making his grand entrance into Camelot. Galahad appears as both the physical and spiritual embodiment of perfection, combining the physical prowess of his father Lancelot with the spiritual character of his mother, one of the keepers of the Grail. At the heart of the tale is an empty seat at the Round Table that in other tales had been kept empty in remembrance of Judas Iscariot. This time it becomes the Siege Perilous, a seat where no knight has yet been able to sit without dire consequences. When Galahad enters Camelot, the inscription over the seat now declares this to be Galahad's seat.

Furthermore, the legend surrounding the sword Excalibur and the stone that in other Arthurian tales comes to be associated with Arthur and his rightful place on the throne appears here with Galahad as the hero. On the day of his arrival, after both of these miraculous events have occurred, the knights gather around the Round Table and take their seats. Then they hear a clap of thunder and become unable to speak as the Holy Grail appears, levitating before them and lighting up the entire room as if the sun was shining indoors. The Grail served the choicest food before each of the knights before it mysteriously vanished.

Painting of Sir Galahad by George Frederick Watts

After this experience, five of the knights vow to seek the Grail: Gawain; Lancelot; Perceval; Bors; and Galahad. The author portrays Gawain as the most sinful of the group, and he becomes frustrated in his lack of success with his quest, even though his misadventures make for good storytelling. After his own series of adventures, Lancelot eventually makes his way to a deserted chapel, where he can just make out the Grail sitting on a silver table as he peers through a locked grille. Exhausted from his prior adventures, he falls asleep at the most inopportune time. While he sleeps, a squire brings an injured knight in on a litter before the Grail, where the knight receives healing. As they leave, the squire tells him that the sleeping knight must have committed some grave sin in order to miss seeing the miraculous healing accomplished by the Grail.

Later on, Lancelot arrives at Corbenic at midnight and enters a chapel that housed the Holy Grail, where he sees a vision of various angels preparing the Eucharist and various other rites associated with the mass. When the priest lifted up the host to consecrate it, Lancelot saw two men standing above the priest's hands on either side, and they appeared to be placing a third, younger boy into the priest's arms. The priest looked like he was about ready to topple over from the weight, and forgetting that he had been warned not to come any closer, Lancelot rushed to steady the priest. As soon as he moved forward, Lancelot was struck unconscious by a fiery blast from heaven. He remained in that state for 24 days, and his quest for the Grail was over.

The three remaining knights then make their way to Corbenic. Before entering Corbenic, Galahad opens the tomb of his ancestor Simeon, who is thereby freed from the flames of purgatory. Nine other knights from the realm join these three, and together, the 12 knights then witness a heavenly communion similar to that aborted by the impetuous act of Lancelot. This time, the priest who begins the process is Josephus, whom this tradition believes to be the first Christian bishop. After making all the preparations, Josephus has the knights sit round a table and then disappears. It is then that Jesus steps out of the Grail, and he then continues officiating the mass where Josephus had left off. The 12 knights watch in awe as each receives this other-worldly communion.

***How Sir Galahad, Sir Bors and Sir Perceval were Fed with the Sanc Grael; But Sir Perceval's Sister Died by the Way*, by Dante Gabriel Rossetti (1864)**

It is at this point in the story that the author puts his take on the nature and history of the Grail. He does this by having Jesus ask Galahad about the Grail, allowing him to answer his own question when Galahad refuses to answer it. Speaking in the third person, Jesus identifies the Grail as the platter which held the paschal lamb eaten by Jesus and his disciples at the Last Supper. This is only slightly different from Robert de Boron's take, which was that the Grail had held the bread that Jesus broke at the Last Supper. After explaining the mystery of the Grail, Jesus then commissions them to take the Grail from Logres to a spiritual palace in Sarras.

After another adventure fighting the pagan king of Sarras, Galahad becomes king and then dies having fulfilled his quest. Upon his death. the hand of God descends to scoop up the Grail and the bleeding lance, ushering them both up to heaven. Perceval then retires to the life of a hermit, and Bors alone rides on to Camelot to inform Arthur and his court of their adventures with the Grail.

The Grail story had become so popular in France that it spread to Germany as well, and a knight named Wolfram von Eschenbach decided to write his own novel about the Grail in German for his patron, Count Hermann of Thuringia. Because of the translation of the name from French into German, scholars refer to his final work as *Parzival*. Wolfram was a very accomplished writer and spends a great deal of time on the back-story of Perceval, detailing the various knightly exploits of his father and brothers. When his story reaches the point where Chrétien's had begun, Wolfram followed the former's story quite closely, with a few minor timeline changes and differences in emphasis. One of these slight differences was that there were many knights feasting at the Grail castle along with Perceval.

However, the big differences, at least regarding the Grail, appear in the monk's explanation to Perceval of the nature of the Grail. The monk calls those knights who dined in the hall of the Fisher King "templars." He then goes on to explain that they receive their food from a stone, called *lapsit exillis* in Latin. The stone prevents people from aging and brings out their most striking and beautiful features. Others call this stone the Grail, according to Wolfram. The monks proceeds to explain that the stone itself summons knights and ladies to itself while they are yet children, and the stone also acts as a stele, containing the names and lineage of those whom it summons. As soon as each reads their own name and lineage upon the stone, that writing vanishes from the face of the stone.

About 200 years later, this Grail tradition began to spread to the English-speaking world. Henry Lovelich translated *The Lancelot-Grail Cycle* into English as *The History of the Holy Grail* around 1450. About a generation later, Thomas Malory wrote his *Morte d'Arthur*, which was published in 1485. The subject of the Holy Grail, along with other Arthurian themes and legends has captivated English readers and audiences, ever since.

Modern Conceptions Regarding the Origins of the Grail Legend

Since the 19th century, literary scholars have sought the source of the Grail legend, and in *The Search for the Holy Grail: Scholars, Critics and Occultists* (2002), Juliette Wood provided a good summary of the scholarship related to the grail over the past two centuries. One of the points that scholars picked up on immediately was the wide variation in the description of the physical appearance of the Grail. They tried to account for this variation by making reference to literary models where they had seen this same phenomenon occur. The model that most appealed to 19th century scholars was that of an original source document or even a stream of tradition. These scholars knew that when authors have an enigmatic original source that allows for multiple interpretations, they might use the same source but come up with several different interpretations. Since many of the writers of the Grail novels, including Chrétien, actually referred to source manuscripts that they had either found or had been given to them, this became the prevailing paradigm in Grail novel scholarship during the 19th century. Thus, their main task was attempting to find the original enigmatic source that could account for the various depictions of the Grail in the French novels.

One prime example of a 19th century medieval scholar was Alfred Nutt. Since many of the elements contained in the Arthurian legends had pagan Celtic roots that were then baptized and rebranded as Christian legends, Nutt believed that the same development would hold true for the

Holy Grail. As a folklorist, he believed that oral tradition was a more reliable means of accessing the ancient past than written records were. Therefore, he scoured the local collections of Irish, Welsh and Scottish Gaelic folktales for any mention of magical vessels or heroes seeking supernatural objects of some kind. He also made reference to the medieval texts in these languages with similar themes. This trend continued throughout the first half of the 20th century.

The problem with each of these types of analyses is that they would focus their attention on only one conceptualization of the Grail and ignore all others. For example, one of the myths in Nutt's work, *The Holy Grail with Especial Reference to its Celtic Origin* (1888), focuses on a food-producing vessel that is an element in a larger Celtic agricultural myth. Such a myth might help to explain the Grail as described in the first continuation, but Nutt would be hard pressed to explain how such a myth lay at the source of the poems about the Grail by Chrétien and Robert de Boron. In fact, the ease with which folkloric traditions from various societies can be connected with the themes in the Grail novels is apparent in a series of articles published in the Journal of American Folklore in the late 1970's. In those articles, C. Scott Littleton sought to demonstrate that folkloric traditions found among the Sarmatian communities in the Caucus mountains were the true source of the Grail legends.

Another conception regarding the Holy Grail origins began with conspiracy theorists in the 1970's and 80's. A group of three friends and novelists seized on the group that appears at the very end of the cycle of French novels concerning the Grail - the Templars - as the source for the Grail legends (Baigent, Leigh, and Lincoln, 1982). They conflated this group, formed as a holy order of knights only a generation or so before Chrétien began writing, with the descendants of Joseph of Arimathea, who guarded the Grail in unbroken succession. According to Wolfram von Eschenbach, who introduced them to the Grail tradition, this was the name for the knights who sought the Grail, not of its guardians. They then combined this Templar conception with the rumor of the buried treasure that Saunière, a 19th century priest, found in Rennes-le-Château. This they then overlaid with a fanciful reparsing of the French phrase *san gréal* (Holy Grail) as *sang réal* ("royal blood"). In turn, this theory, presented in the 1982 book *The Holy Blood and the Holy Grail*, provided inspiration for Dan Brown's best-selling novel *The Da Vinci Code*.

However, the linguistic mistakes in this popular and fanciful etymology are egregious. The Latin word *rēgal(um)* that lies behind the English word "royal" had already become *royal* in Old French, which is where English borrowed the word from in the first place. The sound rule that changes long /e/ in Vulgar Latin to the diphthong /oi/ in Old French only occurs in French, as does the loss of the consonant /g/ in between vowels. If the word were Latin, it would require a /g/ and appear as *sang rēgal* and if it were Old French, it would have to be *sang royal*. In other words, the phrase *sang réal* would be meaningless in Vulgar Latin and in Old French. All of this is beside the fact that the term "Grail" is not paired with the adjective "holy" until quite late in the development of the tradition, and that the earliest mentions of the "Grail" are actually spelled *graal.*

Of course, the fun thing about historical fiction is that the science, linguistic or otherwise, does not have to be accurate. It just has to sound convincing. And in the mouth of the character Dr. Robert Langdon, this fanciful etymology sure sounds scientific and convincing. Viewed in this light, readers might even liken Dan Brown to the authors who followed Chrétien, carrying on the ancient tradition of the Grail novel as developed by the French, complete with the quest of the hero and the reimagining of the shape and character of the Grail itself.

Bibliography

Baigent, Michael, Richard Leigh and Henry Lincoln. *The Holy Blood and the Holy Grail.* London, 1982.

Barb, A. A. "The Round Table and the Holy Grail." *Journal of the Warburg and Courtald Institutes* 19 (1956) 40-67.

Barber, Richard. *The Holy Grail: Imagination and Belief.* Cambridge, MA, 2004.

Brown, Arthur C. L. "The Bleeding Lance." *Publications of the Modern Language Association of America* 25 (1910) 1-59.

Brown, Dan. *The Da Vinci Code*. New York, 2003.

[*Joseph d'Arimathea*] *Joseph of Arimathea: A Critical Edition*. Ed. David Lawton. New York, 1983.

Littleton, C. Scott. "The Holy Grail, the Cauldron of Annwn, and the Nartyamonga: A Further Note on the Samartian Connection." *The Journal of American Folklore* No. 365 (1979) 326-33.

Littleton, C. Scott and Ann C. Thomas. "The Samartian Connection: New Light on the Origin of the Arthurian and Holy Grail Legends." *The Journal of American Folklore* No. 359 (1978) 513-27.

Newell, William Wells. "The Legend of the Holy Grail. I. The Perceval of Crestien." *The Journal of American Folklore* No. 37 (1897) 117-34.

Newell, William Wells. “The Legend of the Holy Grail. II.” *The Journal of American Folklore* No. 38 (1897) 217-32.

Newell, William Wells. “The Legend of the Holy Grail. III.” *The Journal of American Folklore* No. 39 (1897) 299-312.

Newell, William Wells. “The Legend of the Holy Grail. IV.” *The Journal of American Folklore* No. 40 (1898) 39-54.

Newell, William Wells. “The Legend of the Holy Grail. V.” *The Journal of American Folklore* No. 46 (1899) 189-207.

Newell, William Wells. “The Legend of the Holy Grail. VI.” *The Journal of American Folklore* No. 47 (1899) 275-83.

Newell, William Wells. “The Legend of the Holy Grail. VII.” *The Journal of American Folklore* No. 56 (1902) 54-55.

Nutt, Alfred. *Studies in the Legend of the Holy Grail: with especial reference to the hypothesis of its Celtic origin.* London, 1888.

[*Perlesvaus*] *The High Book of the Grail.* Trans. Nigel Bryant. Cambridge, NJ, 1978.

Roach, William. “Transformations of the Grail Theme in the First Two Continuations of the Old French ‘Perceval’.” *Proceedings of the American Philosophical Society* 110 (1966) 160-64.

Wood, Juliette. “The Search for the Holy Grail: Scholars, Critics and Occultists.” *Proceedings of the Harvard Celtic Colloquium* 22 (2002) 226-48.

Manufactured by Amazon.ca
Bolton, ON